Earth Government: A blueprint for a radical new future.

DEDICATIONS

To God. May we prove to You our ability as humankind to live at peace with one another and to be the good custodians of planet Earth that You so want us to be; that by our very actions we persuade You from bringing Your wrath and judgement upon us and allow humanity to spread Your Word across the stars.

To every human being past, present and future. Our current generation owes you our total and unreserved energy to protect all your legacies, hopes, dreams and desires for an enlightened human race and a better home planet at peace with itself.

To my wife and children for their continuous love, support and guidance, without which I could not have written this book

CONTENTS

FOREWORD

"The government of the earth is in the hands of the Lord, He sets the right man over it at the right time." Ecclesiasticus 10:4

On February 17th, 1950, James Paul Warburg confidently declared to the United States Senate: "We shall have world government, whether or not we like it. The only question is whether world government will be achieved by conquest or consent."[1]

In his three day visit to Denmark … "Mr. Winston Churchill last night called for the creation of a World super-government, with Russia as one of its pillars. In a major broadcast speech before an audience of 5,000 he said the prospects for peace and human progress were dark and doubtful, unless some form of effective world super-government could be set up and brought into action quickly."[2] Winston Churchill. The Canberra Times, Friday 13th October 1950.

Interestingly, I began scoping out the detail of a future Earth Government in 2007 with the creation of www.earthgovernment.net – the Earth Government twitter account came online much later in 2014. Clearly the 2007 launch of the official website pre-dated many recent world events, including the world economic crash of 2008, the election of Barack Obama as the 44th US President, the war in Syria, the so called 'Brexit' vote which witnessed the desire of the British people to leave the European Union and the election of Donald J Trump as the 45th US President.

---

[1] http://www.spingola.com/new_world_order1.htm
[2] https://trove.nla.gov.au/newspaper/article/2803089

I often reflect upon where the world would be now had an Earth Government took off right from the offset in 2007. Would we be living on a much more stable and greener planet, where hunger and war are confined to history, and on a planet which offers greater freedoms for people to travel and to trade, and to coin a post Donald Trump election phrase, a World without walls but with bridges. Or put another way a World with boundaries but without borders.

In its simplistic form the 20th century will go down in the history books as the century of global wars between nationalistic super powers. Within the confines of just one hundred years humanity witnessed two World Wars (1914-1918 and 1939-1945), the Russian civil war (1917-1922), the Irish war of independence (1919-1921), the Cold War (1947-1991), the Korean war (1950-1953), the Kenya emergency (1952-1960), the Falklands war (1982), the Gulf war (1990-1991), the Rwandan Civil War (1990 to 1994) and the Bosnian war (1992-1995) to name just a few.

In addition the world witnessed the creation and use of the nuclear bomb and other weapons of mass destruction including chemical and biological warfare, genocide in Africa, and conflict in the Middle East. It is suggested[3] that military conflict took place in every single year during the 20th century with an estimated loss of life of 187 million people - the equivalent of more than 10% of the world's population in 1913, although this figure is likely to be on the conservative side. And I find myself asking what if just one of those 187 million people who died in conflict was another Einstein or Beethoven or Steve Jobs. How much that one person would have contributed to the betterment of

---

[3] https://www.theguardian.com/education/2002/feb/23/artsandhumanities.highereducation. Eric Hobsbawm.

humanity. It just proves that when we fight one another we are literally shooting ourselves in the foot – pun intended.

In contrast, I argue the 21st century will be divided into three distinct periods – global terrorism, the fight for democracy & freedoms and a time of suffering and conflict resulting from climatic change.

We have already seen from the attack on the Twin Towers in New York on 11th September 2001 (9/11) instrumented by Al Qaeda to the rise of Islamic State in 2015 the dawn of the age of the terrorist and the suicide bomber.

It is suggested that one person's terrorist can also be another person's freedom fighter. We must not forget the acts of war inflicted upon countries such as Iraq, Afghanistan and Libya by the USA, Russia and European, which could be argued, contributed to much of this hatred and violence in the first place.

The Arab spring that spread across the Middle East and North Africa in 2010 and more recently the protests in Hong Kong against Chinese authoritarian rule are current examples of those hoping for greater democracy and individual human freedoms which many in the West take for granted. As you know these protests were eventually quashed by their respective governments but not without significant consequences; particularly in Syria, Libya and Yemen. In a way these protests played into the hands of so called terrorists but also enabled already hard line governments to use these as a means to extend their authoritarian rule and remove many societal freedoms. What other global fights for democracy will the 2020's, the 2030's and the 2040's bring?

And in terms of climatic change, we are only now beginning to feel its initial effects, through recent wide scale planetary floods and droughts. Our planet will soon enter a phase of accelerated climate change with year on year heat waves and extreme flooding. The planet's air is the most polluted of all time, the continued use of plastic has entered our own food chain from the oceans and the soil. Population displacement is at record levels chiefly as a result of war but with a changing climate will only accentuate.

According to the UNHCR[4] - measured against the Earth's current (2015) 7.349 billion population … suggests that 1 in every 113 people globally (65.3 million people) is now either an asylum-seeker, internally displaced or a refugee – a level of risk for which UNHCR knows no precedent.

In addition, according to the World Wildlife Foundation (WWF), planet Earth has lost half of its wildlife in the last 40 years[5]. Humanity's relentless assault on the natural living world is beyond what it can tolerate. And the problem can't be blamed on one country alone – it is a human induced scenario caused by rapid urbanization and a deep thirst by humankind to exploit as much of the planet's resources as possible for profit.

So what can be done and what does this book intend to achieve? Well, I want to provide a new narrative – a narrative which can set humanity on a different path – an enlightened path. I want to be clear from the outset, this book is not about politics, but rather a steer towards better leadership of people and better management of our planet's resources.

---

[4] http://www.unhcr.org/afr/news/press/2016/6/5763ace54/1-human-113-affected-forced-displacement-hits-record-high.html
[5] https://www.theguardian.com/environment/2014/sep/29/earth-lost-50-wildlife-in-40-years-wwf

Our present journey will only lead to our eventual destruction, and we must not allow that to happen. I and many others too, believe it is our destiny to thrive as a species but we can only do so if we dramatically change our mind set to how we can live in harmony within our environment; and this ranges from our smallest of villages, up to our towns and cities and on a global pan continental scale. In other words we must 'green up' our urban areas, not just providing tree vegetation but also crop bearing trees and areas we can grow vegetables to feed local communities. Moreover, I set humanity a task for every household which has a garden to have a vegetable patch. Just imagine the environmental not to mention the health benefits of that happening.

Humanity must also unite under one banner and live in peace. Differences have to be settled once and for all with a common goal championed across every nation. A goal to impart the creation of the new human empire. Yes, this is a utopian dream but surely it's a dream worth striving for if it will mean the survival of our planet and its multitude of species, including the human species.

INTRODUCTION

"Every civilisation in the world has ultimately collapsed. It would be very hubristic to think we will be the only civilization to survive."
Homer

As already mentioned there are three significant global issues affecting humanity at the present time – terrorism, the fight for democracy and climate change, and I would like to discuss each as succinctly as possible.

The rise of terrorism in the twenty first century has taken many by surprise. It has been portrayed as originating from an organized, well-funded group determined to cause maximum loss of life. In general terms we are led to believe it is the rise of the Islamic fundamentalist waging holy jihad against the infidels. And this in part probably has some truth – although truth depends upon a certain point of view. It is very much true that a minority of Muslims are seeking answers on the far right of their beliefs; but so too are those in western Christian countries, where we have witnessed the resurgence of far right anti-foreigner extremist groups.

However, I would argue that what we have seen since 2001 is the rise of disillusionment, a lack of hope and a lack of imagination caused by failings of socio-economic and political systems across the globe, mainly affecting our youth.

In a perverse sort of way all our national governments have contributed to our present circumstances by alienating certain sectors of our civilizations. Politicians around the world always seem to have the knack of implementing policies which are either divisive or ostracise specific groups within our societies. So I put it to you the reader that we must change this approach and this book sets out how we can achieve the unity we so badly crave and need.

In terms of the future fight for democracy, we have already seen the power of the so called Arab Spring uprisings, and whilst these have not yet resulted in the change some may have wanted, there will be other rallying calls for greater representation, justice and democracy. We may even see nations fighting non-nuclear ideological wars especially on the Korean peninsula with both North and South Korea in a World War two combat situation with tanks and troops on the ground. Governments of south American countries may embark on campaigns to acquire more land. We may even see war in Europe once again!

The last few decades have seen a growing media appetite in the discussion around climate change and how this will affect the planet and human civilization. Conferences such as the Copenhagen Conference in 2009; the South American conference of Caucan in 2011; the Rio +20 conference in 2012; the Paris conference in 2015 as well as numerous G20 meetings, all of which seem to have failed. Only the Paris talks in 2015[6] came away with any kind of meaningful agreement but even this was not binding and it seemed that it took twenty years to get to that point! Indeed, the Paris 2015 conference only agreed the target – not the way or ways each country would achieve that target. And with Donald Trump, now elected as the 45th

---

[6] The Paris climate conference (COP21) in December 2015, 195 countries adopted the first-ever universal, legally binding global climate deal. https://ec.europa.eu/clima/policies/international/negotiations/paris_en

President of the United States, it looks as if the USA will now back out of this agreement, leaving the path open for even greater climatic disasters and a furtherance of accelerated climate change.

It is clear that any changes in our climate – whether regional or global - will have a serious impact upon us all, just as pollution created in one country can have adverse effects upon another country upwind. It is well evidenced that climate change is being caused by human activity. The point is accepted that the climate has always changed on our planet over millennia but it has never previously happened within a hundred years or so, which is the case today.

I put it to you that climate change will be humanity's Armageddon. It will result in the melting of the polar regions, changing of the Gulf stream, a change in the El Nino, mass species extinction, rising sea levels, drowning of lowland coastal areas, depleted freshwater reserves, reduction in agricultural capacity, mass human migration, famine, civil and international wars.

The human race is on the brink of disaster if it carries on in the way it is at the moment both in terms of fighting one another as well polluting our own home world. We must act now and we must act as if we were at war - a war for survival and for peace.

CHAPTER 1 - WHERE ARE WE NOW?

"Humanity must push forward at all times but not at all cost." Wayne
Pritchard (2018).

Whilst terrorism and climate change will be the most significant
contemporary world issues in the 21st century, they are not by far the
only ones which humankind has to deal with. Natural disasters, failing
economies, mass migration, extreme poverty, famine, AIDS/HIV, world
debt, lack of drinking water, energy security, international disputes,
confused tiers of government, corruption, unacceptable
unemployment, an electoral apathy towards political systems,
intolerable racism, child labour, female oppression, child labour,
human trafficking, slavery, dictatorships and crimes against humanity
to name just a few.

These are real significant issues which humanity has to wake up to
and resolve. And whilst it is acknowledged a great many people and
organizations are working tirelessly to make a difference towards
ending human suffering, these strategic issues lack real global
leadership.

"Humanity is quick to adapt but slow to learn." Wayne Pritchard *(2017).*

The United Nations (UN) has worked well over recent decades and its role in shaping a post war world will be recorded in history as a great success. Indeed, the UN was meant to lay the foundations for future greater political and economic integration but has sadly become stagnated and bureaucratic. Unfortunately, the current global problems faced by humanity at this present time will never be solved by the world institutions as they exist in their current form.

The question you are probably now asking yourself is how another political organization can make any kind of difference.

The answer is simple - political stream lining, defining a new strategic plan for humankind and global co-ordination towards a new fair, social Capimmunism, equal and Green Economy - one in which respects, promotes and preserves individual national cultures as well providing a much needed vision for humanity. As it is said - we can only grow if we know our roots.

Current national governments are not addressing our global problems or helping their people; they have failed! Many are illegitimate dictatorships and any attempts at International conferences, i.e. G8, G20; either fails to deliver upon promises made or is too elitist by excluding smaller countries. The consequences of no action are and will be disastrous.

Unemployment, especially amongst the youth, is at record levels and is now totally unacceptable. We need to be in a position where we see ourselves having a role in society as opposed to just a job!

The vision, therefore, is to reduce our current political governance structure into a more simplistic form. Each country requires specific national governance and I propose countries should be governed by an elected leadership team of around 30 individuals - with an exact 50/50 male to female ratio as well as adhering to the ethnic percentage makeup of the country which the leadership team represents. Each member of the leadership team will need to be experts in the field they are leading on, so for example – a finance minister would need to come from a previous financial or banking role, an environmental minister would need to have experience in environmental or ecological issues. Membership of such a leadership team would only be for a fixed term of around three years and no one individual would be allowed to undertake more than the two terms in office. I would like to involve a great number of young people / children into this leadership team where individuals have shown a demonstrable enthusiasm in a particular field. The leader of the leadership team him/her self would be directly elected and this role would be the direct link of the country into the Earth Government.

I also envisage the possibility of each of our six inhabited continents having its own grand committee to assist each country within the continent it represents. Clearly, there would be a challenge with Australia, which by its very nature as a country as well as a continent would have both a leadership team and a grand committee or could find its path as a member of a wider Pacific Ocean grand committee. Again, membership to this would be elected and ideally draw upon those individuals who have shone in their role on the leadership team and earned a promotion to the grand committee.

The six leaders from the six grand committees would in themselves provide the basis for the new global security council and would have certain global responsibilities including providing a checks and balances approach to the role of the Earth President and providing that group of individuals who act as the Commander in Chief role of the global defence force. The role of the Earth President would become an elected position and would be a shared responsibility between one elected male and one elected female, and ideally representative of different colour and religion. This role, for the purposes of clarity, would not have direct rule over any armed forces.

Election funding for the leadership teams, the grand committees or the Earth President will either be through a central Earth Government fund or entirely self-funded. Candidates will be able to access a 0% loan which will be re-payable over the 5 year election term. There will be a ceiling on the amount which can be borrowed or spent in any election. Candidates will be authorised to obtain donations to assist the repayment of the loan. These donations must be small in amount, limited by donor, audited and published. Non-payment of loans from previous election campaigns will result in the disqualification of these candidates standing in future elections leading to imprisonment in cases of non-co-operation and fraud. Candidates will only be allowed to have two terms in office thus preventing the career politician and ensuring younger blood is brought in the political sphere.

This will result in a streamlined system offering quite phenomenal savings together with accessible democracy for all.

We also need news services around the world to be free to report on all issues and to be fully independent from government. I want journalists to be the eyes and ears of the Earth Government.

What we must remember is that:

"People shouldn't be afraid of their government. Governments should be afraid of their people."[7]

---

[7] Alan Moore. https://www.goodreads.com/quotes/8065-people-shouldn-t-be-afraid-of-their-government-governments-should-be

CHAPTER 3 – EARTH LEGISLATION

A future Earth Government would seek to establish the following legislation (although not in any particular order): Most if not all of these will be discussed in much fuller detail throughout the remainder of this book.

1. An Earth Peace Treaty
2. Legislation for the creation of Earth Law
3. An Earth Human Right Charter
4. A Global Clean Air Charter
5. A Global Nuclear Missile Disarmament Charter
6. A Global Free Movement of People Charter
7. A Global Free Trade Charter
8. An Earth Health Service Charter
9. A Global Energy Charter
10. An Earth Education Charter
11. A Global Waste Sanitation Charter
12. A Global Clean Water / Oceans Charter
13. An Earth Science, R+D and Innovation Charter
14. An Earth Defence Charter
15. An Earth Rapid Response + Emergencies Charter
16. An Earth Coastguard Charter
17. An Earth plastic minimization Charter
18. A Global Security and Intelligence Charter
19. A Global Transport Charter
20. A Global Social Infrastructure + Improvement Charter
21. An Earth Justice and Penal Reform Charter
22. An Earth Space Agency Charter
22. A Global Data Protection Charter

CHAPTER 4 – A NEW ECONOMIC STRATEGY

"Education is the best economic policy there is." Tony Blair

Much has been written recently concerning a new kind of global economics. It is clear that our current ways of trading and doing business at a macro level just simply isn't working. We seem to be functioning within a capitalistic system that is in overdrive and one in which benefits the few and not the majority. A new global Economic Strategy will be put in place which will adhere to the principles of fairness, least environmental impact and opportunity for all.

There will be a new single tax system. No tax will be levied on purchases but only on income, therefore an abolishment of Value Added Tax (VAT).

New tax thresholds on income must be established. No tax will be paid on income up to £10,000 GBP, and then a graded system at specific intervals. There will be 11% tax on £11,000, 12% on £12,000 13% on £13,000, 14% on £14,000, and so on up to 20% from £20,000 to £45,000. 30% tax will be levied on incomes from £46,000 to £99,000. 40% tax will be levied on those earning in excess of £100,000 up to £499,000. 50% tax for those earning between £500,000 to £999,000. Those earning greater than £1 million will be taxed at the 75% threshold and 95% for earnings over £5 million. Clearly these amounts will vary over time due to inflationary pressures and also according to each country but it's the principle that I wish to convey at this stage.

Everyone will pay the same tax whatever country they are registered to so we avoid the problem of non-domiciles and so called tax havens.

All such tax avoidance schemes will be outlawed by a future Earth Government.

There will be a unified business rate tax calculated upon turnover, profit and the number of employees within the organization; therefore multi-national companies employing many thousands of people will clearly pay more than much smaller businesses. Tax rates will be set around 20% for multinationals and 5% for sole traders. Medium sized companies would be looking at paying around 10% tax. We must end the current perversion where global organizations such as Amazon pay such low amounts of tax compared to their actual turnover.

There will be a standard interest rate of between 0%-5% for saving and between 0%-7% for borrowing, fixed for around 5 years for all country's and organizations and then re-reviewed every 5 years.

Consideration should be given to a single global currency, measured in Earth Credits or a system based on regional / continental currencies so that the planet ends up with around 10 or so global currencies. Whilst this is admitted to be an ideal it is in no way a prerequisite or indeed a barrier to forming an Earth Government.

There must be an Earth minimum wage which will reduce poverty and produce an equalisation of production costs. There will essentially be an Earth maximum wage which will see a tax threshold of 95% at any income earned above £5 million GBP or equivalent according to the country.

A new universal seamless work based Pension system will be set up which will guarantee every person a fair income in old age. Each person's pension will follow them through their career path as a pension brief case. It will be funded by annual contributions of around 5% of those in employment; and 2.5% employer contributions. Those who have not worked will still obtain a pension, albeit at a reduced level compared with those who have made contributions to their pension provision. This must be administered at a country level and overseen by the country's leadership team.

Every country will be tasked to diversify their current economies to include an equal three way split between agricultural production (30%), manufacturing (30%) and service industries (30%). Other entrepreneurial industries will make up the remaining 10%. It is only through a re-balancing of our economies across all countries will we safeguard against the current global boom bust economics we currently witness every 10 to 20 years.

There must be an aim to achieve zero unemployment across the whole planet. It is estimated that around 6%[8] of the world's eligible working population are unemployed. But there are wide country wide variations hidden in this figure with some countries being as high as 25% to 30%. Put simply the World is not working with so many people under-utilized. Job creation in our countries and especially youth unemployment will be addressed through economic diversification, the creation of new global agencies such as health, education, emergency and rescue, house building, recycling, coastguard and space agency. The construction of better sanitation and an Earth Electrical Grid will provide jobs for decades to come.

[8] https://data.worldbank.org/indicator/SL.UEM.TOTL.ZS?view=chart

In terms of global lottery companies, an Earth Government would tax all winnings by individuals and syndicates. A suggested tax of 10% would be levied and this could raise £10 billion GBP a year.

Furthermore, an Earth Government will provide a paid salary for one parent to care for a child up to the age of 5 on their first born only; thus ensuring society recognises the full and proper part parents, and in particular mothers, play in bringing up children. The salary would be calculated at a country level and in partnership with the Earth Government and a country's leadership team. A review would undoubtedly take place after a decade or so to see if the scheme is working or could be extended to include the first two children in a family.

CHAPTER 5 – EARTH TRADE STRATEGY

Sooner or later every war of trade becomes a war of blood."
Eugene V. Debs

A global Trade Strategy will provide a total commitment to trading freely and fairly between all countries, helping to reduce our use of carbon (even to the point that we become carbon negative), providing greater emphasis on local produce for local people and the establishment of an Earth minimum wage and a maximum wage.

There must be tariff free trade where possible across all countries and sectors. Clearly there is a caveat to that in which those products or materials that create environmental damage must either incur a tariff or be outlawed all together.

Economic development of every country must be supported to alleviate poverty but must be done in an environmentally sustainable way. Earth trade must be based from now on, on a new Earth Economic model, which has already been scoped out in detail by other key writers[9]. One of the first tasks of any future Earth Government would be to establish a working commission to work out how best we can develop a new global economic model.

An Earth Government will work towards a consistent food labelling system so that consumers in every country can be assured of what their food is made of and where their food has come from. And in line with the agricultural strategy we must ensure that our food security is

---

[9]https://scholar.google.co.uk/scholar?
q=a+new+global+economic+model&hl=en&as_sdt=0&as_vis=1&oi=scholart&sa=X&ved=0ahUKEwjTvPOEyd
PZAhULLMAKHSA9CjoQgQMILDAA

assured but is also wholesome when produced. I'll probably repeat myself later but we need to transition away from the intensification of farming to a more extensive approach.

A standard symbol for representing vegetarian food will also be rolled out across all appropriate food producers. And there must be a greater drive to encourage each and every one of us to eat less meat. We know that our meat production is damaging our planet in so many ways – grain is grown to feed livestock, cattle and other animals are producing CO2, and on top of that we're cutting down more and more of our tropical rainforests to graze cattle. We seem to have caught ourselves in this environmentally destructive feedback loop and an Earth Government would end this cycle.

To conclude this chapter, I firmly believe every country can trade in a much smarter way that ensures all citizens have fair access to goods and services but also in a way that contributes to future carbon negative goals.

CHAPTER 6 – EARTH ENERGY STRATEGY

"It is time for a sustainable energy policy which puts consumers, the environment, human health and peace first." Dennis Kucinich

It is imperative that humanity has a global energy strategy with renewable energy sources at its core. The planet requires an urgent programme of mass production and installation of wind farms and solar panel plants on land and at sea, so that we cut carbon emissions by 90% of present levels by 2025. However, even that may not be enough to quench our thirst for electricity, and in short the only long term viable plan is in the development of a new energy source.

It is admirable that in 2018 we are finally moving to electric vehicles, but this will only put more pressure on the power stations to burn more fossil fuels in order to generate the electricity needed to power the electric vehicles. Current thinking of electrical generation is insular and in non-coherent. Humanity requires a strategy that ensures that electrical supply is greater than demand. With that in mind two simple ideas must be put in place. Firstly, an Earth Electrical Grid is to be established so that electricity surpluses are transferred to any country of need. This would be a platform of shared cabling infrastructure and managed at a global level by a central monitoring organization. And secondly, our methods of creating electricity must be much closer to the consumer with all houses being fitted with solar panels and small wind turbines. Houses of the future will become much more self-sufficient in the generation and use of electricity. Clearly, this will be more challenging in northern hemisphere countries but the development of battery technology will result in homes being able to store electricity for days that solar light is not available in any great abundance.

Carbon capture technology is to be used on all existing coal power stations for the remainder of their short lifespan. These power stations as well as gas powered stations are to be phased out as soon as alternative energy sources come online and it is envisaged these will be totally phased out by 2030 at the absolute latest. Nuclear power is not a totally renewable resource and is certainly not carbon free, as it creates a huge amount of carbon from the concrete used in its construction. In addition, uranium 235 waste can never be made totally safe and has a half life of around 700 million years. The use of nuclear power may only assist an Earth Government in the short term, in order to prevent shortfalls of electricity across the globe. An Earth Government will look seriously into developing Thorium based nuclear, nuclear fusion technology and hydrogen as a power source; and if these are found safe and successful will use as part of the mix along with renewable sources. Biofuel technology is also not an option as this reduces valuable land which is so urgently required for the production of food, as well contributing to greenhouses gases.

An Earth Government would be against energy extraction which involves Fracking, Gasification, and other forms of fossil fuel usage. I also believe there is no viability in the continued use of Uranium nuclear production.

In summary to conclude this chapter, the planet requires mass development of both macro generation of electricity through solar plants together with micro generation of electricity in people's homes i.e. solar panels, and this must be provided free of charge by an Earth

Government. And as previously stated this technology must be incorporated into the standard build of all future house building projects.

CHAPTER 7 – EARTH HEALTH SERVICE

"Let us be the ones who say we do not accept that a child dies every three seconds simply because he does not have the drugs you and I have. Let us be the ones to say we are not satisfied that your place of birth determines your right for life. Let us be outraged, let us be loud, let us be bold." Brad Pitt

It is every country's necessity to provide health care provision for its citizens and this tends to be achieved through a combination of public funding and private enterprise. Health care spending varies massively per capita and by GDP between countries as indicated by the OECD data below. Clearly, there are significant variations across the board with the USA spending 10,000 USD per person, Switzerland spending just under 7,000 USD per person, and Norway spending 6,000 USD per person. These three countries are the world's largest health care spenders, when private expenditure is added to public spending. Turkey and Mexico are the lowest spenders on health care at just 1,000 USD per person. The OECD average comes in at just below 4,000 USD per person.

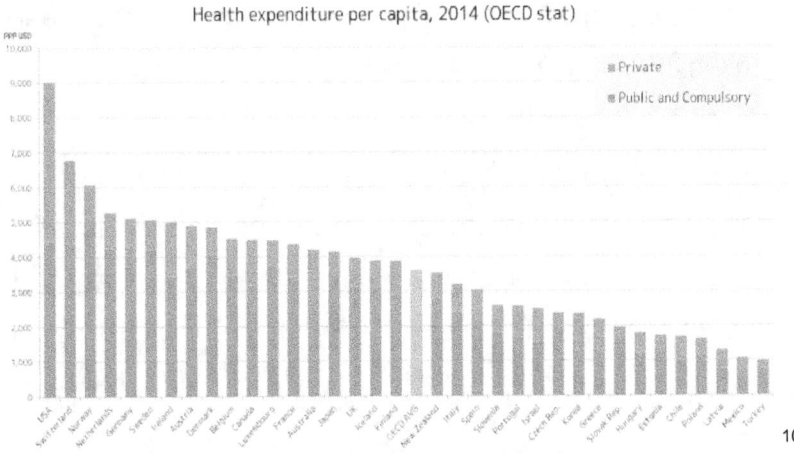

Health expenditure per capita, 2014 (OECD stat)

10

[10] https://commons.wikimedia.org/wiki/File:OECD_health_expenditure_per_capita_by_country.svg

The following table, which is also OECD data, indicates health care spending as a percentage of GDP. It is evident the USA spent around 17% of its GDP on healthcare in 2015, with the UK spending around 10% of its GDP.

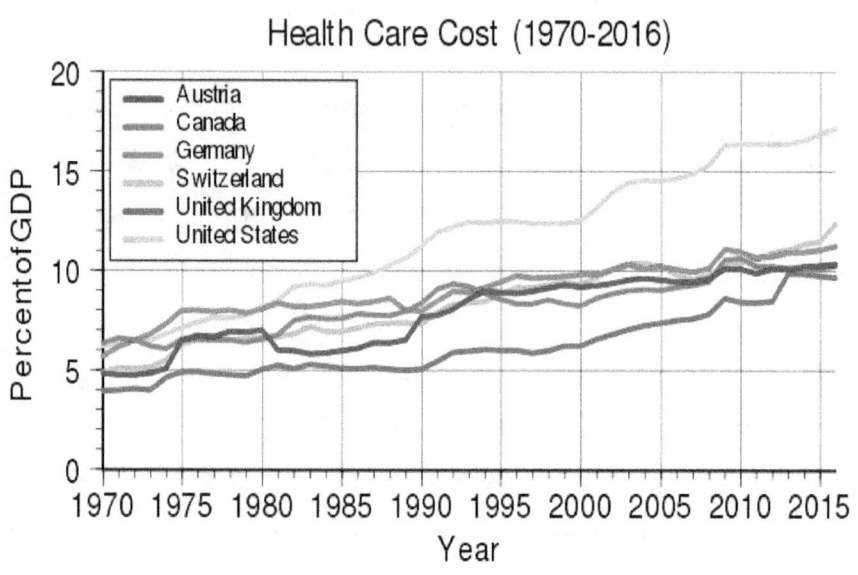

Health Care Cost (1970-2016)

[11]

It is clear therefore, that health care spending across the globe is sporadic to say the least. The creation of an Earth Health Service will ensure a much greater consistency of health care spending – spending which clearly matches each country's requirement.

However, humanity must also focus on the effectiveness of that health care spending so that it is targeted, focussed and produces the best possible outcomes for patients. Mark Britnell, Chairman and Senior Partner, Global Health Practice at KPMG, in his 2016 paper to the

[11] By WikiBasti - Own work, Public Domain, https://commons.wikimedia.org/w/index.php?curid=9820509. Health care cost as percent of GDP (total economy of a nation).

Davos World Economic Forum[12] identified the hallmarks of an efficient health service. These are:

1. A strong primary care system
2. Greater use of technology to contain costs; and
3. A better allocation of resources.

An Earth Health Service will look into arranging health care systems in a way that maximises cost effectiveness on a country by country basis, as well as ensuring basic health care to every human being on the planet as a human right.

That said, the primary focus of the Earth Health Service, will not just be about financial effectiveness; although clearly we need to strive for the ideal model that works in each country, and this may well be different between countries. No, its primary focus must be to have patient care at its heart - putting the patient first. All too often health care systems are designed around the hospital or the local state boundary rather than the actual communities and people in which it is meant to serve.

The secondary focus of the Earth Health Service would be to provide strategic long term planning and development to ensure longevity of health care provision in all countries. Linked to this would the partnership arrangement that is to be put in place with pharmaceutical companies to guarantee the best possible price for medicines and other drugs through bulk buying.

---

[12] https://www.weforum.org/agenda/2016/04/which-countries-have-the-most-cost-effective-healthcare/

An Earth Health Service must also provide free medicines at point of need – and this approach will have to be fully costed and restricted in the first instance to life saving medicines and basic pain killers.

It is imperative, in the future, for patients to receive greater health provision in their own homes – not just diagnosis of ailments through video calls but actual treatment as well – a scanner that detects, diagnosis and delivers medical treatment in the same way we take a shower in the morning.

There is a need to further resource developing new cures for all cancers and treating AIDS/HIV throughout the world, especially in developing countries. An Earth Government would fund and distribute such medicines. Coordinated work needs to be carried out in addressing so called 'bird flus' and managing pandemics, such Ebola and Zika.

It would be well within the reach of an Earth Government to wipe out malaria through vaccinations and the provision of mosquito nets.

An Earth Government through the Earth Health Service would fund projects to improve sanitation across the globe. Starting first with improving basic sanitation systems in developing countries and moving to a situation whereby waste disposal is carried out through use of microwave technology. Microwave technology has been developed already and could be piloted in developed countries within a few years, thus ending our reliance upon clean water in flushing away waste.

The Earth Health Service must also gravitate towards the provision of clean water, clean air and health education projects. It is imperative humanity addresses the issue of the lack of clean drinking water around the globe. A prime goal for any future Earth Government would be to provide clean water for drinking and bathing to every human being within 5 years. A recent invention in the UK is the 'lifesaver bottle' which converts dirty water into clean water. This is just one example in which new technology can be rolled out in a targeted way to save lives.

Humanity must make a societal shift in its attitude towards those people who are drug users from criminality to those requiring medical help. This will be no easy task and may actually involve legalising some drugs in order to provide them under strict medical supervision. Similar medical assistance must be provided to those with alcohol problems.

So in summary, an Earth Health Service will provide that new global health infrastructure which our countries are literally crying out for. A health infrastructure which puts people first, utilizes economies of scale, addresses the urgent issues affecting humanity today but also preparing and preventing where possible the global health emergencies of the future.

"A nation that destroys its soils destroys itself. Forests are the lungs of our land, purifying the air and giving fresh strength to our people."
Franklin D. Roosevelt

"Welcome to Planet Plastic. The only planet in the galaxy to offer the full plastic pollution experience." Wayne Pritchard 2019

Our current environmental issues are more than just about climate change; although clearly climate change is a most pressing matter. There is a greater broader picture than just being carbon neutral. We need to think about how we can sustainably survive as a species in our own right as well as safeguarding all other forms of life on our planet. Indeed, we need to focus not just on the target of reducing carbon emissions but how we become carbon negative and actually draw down on the amount of carbon currently in the atmosphere.

Greater emphasis must be placed on protecting specific global ecosystems, which in themselves would provide the means for capturing existing atmospheric carbon. We must remember that we can't allow the planet to become too cold either and that temperature equilibrium must always be sought. Equilibrium is the key word here where humanity has to find a greater balance with the natural world around us as well as ensuring the continued viability of our species – not an easy task and certainly one which we have been trying grabble with for many decades now. It is intended that an Earth Government could indeed find this equilibrium or at least achieve something very close.

It would be the responsibility of an Earth Environment Agency to provide the immediate protection of all rainforests, woodlands, polar/perma regions, endangered species and ecosystems with a clear mandate to restore equatorial tropical rainforest boundaries to where they were pre 1950. The continued deforestation of our rainforests has been an environmental injustice. According to Rain-tree.com, one and one-half acres of rainforest are lost every second.[13] And of course it's not just about the trees that are being lost – there's also the loss of species within the rainforest regions as a result of deforestation, loss of potential future medicines and also the loss of indigenous peoples, whose culture and way of life must be protected.

Clean air will be basic human right in the new Human Right Charter and therefore the Earth Government will introduce a Clean Air Charter. All current and future technologies in attaining clean air will be shared amongst all industries and all countries. There has to be a significant reduction of the amount of pollution which our towns and cities contribute if we are to improve the health of all people and the wider health of the planet. Clearly, moving away from petrol and diesel cars, vans, buses and lorries will have a major net benefit, but we must also rethink our approach in relation to having environmentally sound housing stock – including but not limited to a move away from gas heating and great use of solar panels and micro wind turbines and use of large batteries within our buildings to store electricity for use during times of deficiency. Indeed, there has to be much greater synergy between our urban built up areas and planted green areas, whether these are large parks or just simply a row of trees running parallel to or in the centre of each road.

[13] http://www.rain-tree.com/facts.htm

An Earth Environmental Agency will establish a global agricultural strategy which will set out the plans of how the increasing planet's population will be fed well into the 22nd century. It is essential that each country becomes more self-sufficient in food production and indeed more home grown produce is promoted at a micro level.

An Earth Environmental Agency will set up a full and independent inquiry into the suitability of genetically modified crops and stem cell food production. Whilst as the author of this book I'm not terribly convinced by this technology we need to know more intelligence around this science before too much damage is inflicted on natural ecosystems and species.

The Earth Environmental Agency will set up and become responsible for an Earth Recycling Agency where items such as electronics are fixed rather than dumped in landfill. An Earth Environmental Agency would also have responsibility for setting these up and maintaining the recycling centres within each country. The rationale and thinking behind such centres is around fixing products that have been discarded or using their electrical components to make other items. We know, for example, that the typical smartphone handset consists of around 40% metals (predominantly copper, gold, platinum, silver and tungsten), 40% plastics and 20% ceramics and trace materials. An interesting article by techradar.com[14] details the precise elements that go into our smartphones and a clear takeaway for me after reading this article is in the need to re-use these precious materials that have already been mined as they will run out a lot sooner than we think.

---

[14] https://www.techradar.com/news/phone-and-communications/mobile-phones/our-smartphone-addiction-is-costing-the-earth-1299378

Each country must recycle its own waste within it's own national border. It is an intolerable situation that we are transporting and dumping supposed recycled plastic waste on other nations. This current situation whereby countries such as those in Europe have been transporting waste to Asian countries is not acceptable and is only contributing further to climate change. The deception that has occurred to European families who in good faith have sorted plastic waste thinking it was actually earmarked for recycling has been a great travesty of the last decade. Linked to this, one of the tasks to be assigned to the Earth Recycling Agency will be the collection and recycling of all plastic waste currently in our seas and oceans. It is essential that we must begin a massive global clean up operation never witnessed before in humanity's history. The technology exists for large scale plastic collection through the use of balers which can be positioned at the mouth of certain rivers. Research has been carried out that indicates 90% of the plastic entering our oceans comes from just 10 rivers - Eight of them are in Asia: the Yangtze; Indus; Yellow; Hai He; Ganges; Pearl; Amur; Mekong; and two in Africa – the Nile and the Niger.[15]

Clearly, this will not resolve 100% of the current plastic problem, so I propose the creation of the Green Rangers – a new environmental global army of scientists, environmentalists and other volunteers to help in the battle of combatting visible plastic waste, micro plastic waste that is already absorbed in animal species as well as other wide reaching ecological issues. Great work is already happening around the planet to help bird species in removing plastic waste from their

[15] https://www.weforum.org/agenda/2018/06/90-of-plastic-polluting-our-oceans-comes-from-just-10-rivers/

guts. An Earth Government would ensure these organizations and the people involved in this crucial activity are brought into the Green Rangers so that an united and properly funded approach can be created.

Another approach which the Earth Environmental Agency will lead is in relation to ensuring the abolishing of single use plastics, whether they are bags, bottles or containers. It is evident that manufacturers have to revert to using glass, cardboard and paper as viable alternatives. A new approach is certainly required in regard to packaging of foods and flat packed material. We need to find a new substitute for plastic wrapping, foil and polystyrene which are currently destroying our global ecosystem.

It is important to stress at this point that the use of cardboard and paper to replace plastic must be from managed sustainable forests grown specifically for this purpose. It would be an injustice if indigenous rainforests or woodlands were used to supply the cardboard box or paper bag industry. And whilst we'll see an uplift of these new industries we have to ensure the forced decline of plastic producing companies. It would be an inevitable and acceptable loss to witness a halving of raw plastic production by 2025. Whilst utilising more alternatives to replace single use plastic it is clear that this won't resolve the whole issue. A solution which I believe requires further investigation is in assigning a commodity value to a plastic bottle such as one penny or one cent and for the original manufacturer of that bottle to then buy it back from the consumer. This is certainly not a new idea and was a particular practice in the UK back in the 1980's.

The human race needs to rethink its position on airline travel, in terms of cheap holiday flights; and the transportation of food via shipping. Shipping actually causes more carbon emissions than aeroplanes! A global strategy on both must be implemented to reduce carbon emissions. Food production must be more locally focused with far greater emphasis on animal welfare.

Energy efficient lightbulbs and the installation of solar panels and micro wind turbines in homes will be funded by the Earth Government as part of the global energy strategy. These would have clear environmental benefits.

CHAPTER 9 – EARTH EDUCATION AGENCY

"If you are planning for a year, sow rice; if you are planning for a decade, plant trees; if you are planning for a lifetime, educate people."
Chinese Proverb

As we all know education is one of the most important elements of any culture. So what exactly is the current state of education across our planet? Well the answer really is best described in one word – fragmented. In short, we are currently failing the children of our planet.

Every country has its own ideas and strategy in educating its citizens. Some countries are considered to have good education systems, with the top 10 of 2019 in the world being that of the UK, USA, Canada, Germany, France, Australia, Switzerland, Sweden, Japan and the Netherlands[16]. This is not to say other countries aren't providing good education, its just that according to the same research these same countries were in the 2018 top 10 rankings too. Interestingly but probably not that surprising the top 10 worst countries for education in 2016 were Chad, Central African Republic, Niger, Guinea, Mali, Sudan, Benin, Yemen, Afghanistan and Liberia[17]. And clearly, the major emerging economies of China, India and Brazil are somewhere in the middle between the two lists.

An Earth Education Agency will ensure that all schools, especially in developing countries and new emerging economies, are equipped with the necessary resources, such as teachers, buildings, books and

---

[16] https://www.master-and-more.eu/en/top-10-countries-with-the-best-education-systems-in-the-world-for-2019/

[17] https://www.globalcitizen.org/en/content/best-worst-countries-list-education-2016/

computers / technology, to provide every child with a decent, well rounded and rewarding education.

It seems to me that one of the stumbling blocks in the approach of having various education systems is the lack of transferability of qualifications between nation states. I therefore propose investigating the possibility of a standard academic qualification which would have validity in every country. Clearly, this will require careful consideration but it would have obvious benefits for individuals who work across borders in our global economy. Such a qualification would either run parallel with existing qualifications or, depending upon the outcome of the research, replace the current fragmented educational qualifications currently in place.

An Earth Government would commission an independent research group to propose the content of the syllabus, tailoring the need for each country in terms of language, diversity, art, geography and history, as well as meeting the challenges we are going to face and the need to train future generations of doctors, scientists, mathematics and engineers.

We need to think of our planet as a business, ensuring we have the right people, in the right job with the right skill sets and at the right time. And if we haven't got this mix right we need to train and coach people rather than enslaving them to a life of claiming benefits. State benefits have a clear purpose in preventing people from going under the breadline but in many westerns democracies, such as those in Europe, the benefit system has become corrupted. There will always be a need for a benefit system in terms of protecting the most vulnerable in society but it is quite clear that people of a working age and fit enough must always be in a job.

Central to this is the education of girls as well as boys in all countries. The exclusion of girls in our education systems is totally unacceptable and draconian in nature. How can any civilization with hold education and learning from 50% of its population and expect to have any kind of longevity. Our children are our future and we must be wise enough to invest in them.

"Once you have an innovation culture, even those who are not scientists or engineers - poets, actors, journalists - they, as communities, embrace the meaning of what it is to be scientifically literate. They embrace the concept of an innovation culture. They vote in ways that promote it. They don't fight science and they don't fight technology."
Neil deGrasse Tyson

It seems so important to me that that in our interconnected global society we haven't fully embraced the idea of combining our efforts in relation to science, Research & Development and general innovation. An Earth Government would ensure we have a new Agency that joins up our world organizations in this field, ensuring we get value for money out of our investments – that is to say we move away from a culture where we are all working on the same project or idea but in different tangents.

The new Earth Science, R&D and Innovation Agency will employ academics, scientists, industrialists, engineers, inventors and entrepreneurs from around the world to work in partnership developing new technologies and products for the furtherance of all humanity.

There is a clear need today for such an organization. The requirement for new green energy sources, finding cures for cancer and other pan epidemics, research in how we can draw down carbon from our atmosphere, new medicines, new ideas on how to feed a global population of 8 to 9 billion people and new thinking on space technology just to name a few.

Many contemporary commentators discuss the need for a new green revolution. Originally referenced by William S Gaud, in his speech on 8 March 1968, as the administrator of the US Agency for International Development (USAID),[18] the green revolution really signified an agricultural revolution and the development of high yielding crops, pesticides and fertilizers. In addition, history also records Norman Borlaug as the "Father of the Green Revolution."[19]

And whilst these contributions have clearly been important, I would like to suggest that the green revolution in the 21st century is more to do with creating and using new green technology to reduce our global carbon footprint and therefore to ensure humankind's existence into the 22nd century. So really a kind of Green Revolution version 2.0 (GR2).

---

[18] https://en.wikipedia.org/wiki/Green_Revolution
[19] https://en.wikipedia.org/wiki/Norman_Borlaug

"Nationalism is an infantile disease. It is the measles of mankind."
Albert Einstein

It is abundantly clear to me that the root of all our past wars has stemmed from the rise of great nation states, fuelled by a sense of nationalistic pride and ideological factions of their (modern) time. These super and self-confident nation states have led to the rise of empires and then war, either through internal breakup, such as the Roman Empire, or conquest by a greater power or coalition of powers, such as World War One and World War Two.

And of course we know that history has a habit of repeating itself. We might not realise it now in the early part of the 21st century but more war is coming our way. Indeed, humanity always seems to be in a continual perpetuation of micro wars, as I have already alluded to my forward. Even today, as I write this chapter, the USA is currently in a trade war with China[20], Saudi Arabia is at war with Yemen[21], and the UK is at odds with Iran with the seizing of the Stena Impero oil tanker[22].

There's no easy way of saying this but this cycle of conflict has to be broken. It will either be through World War 3 or a realization that no one country actually benefits from having their own military that can quickly turn on its neighbours and also in so many instances turn on its own people.

---

[20] https://outsideinsight.com/insights/trade-wars-us-china-tariff-battle-already-impacting-industries-globally/?gclid=EAlaIQobChMI8t3Jt5zd4wIVC7DtCh3JfQbSEAAYAiAAEgLqv_D_BwE
[21] https://en.wikipedia.org/wiki/Saudi_Arabian-led_intervention_in_Yemen
[22] https://www.bbc.co.uk/news/uk-49053383

Therefore, I propose we have an Earth Defence Force. Such a Defence Force will replace all military resources of all national governments into one centralised command structure, under the control of a reformed global Security Council. The new Security Council will have representation from a much wider group of countries and will include many smaller nations. There is no justification for one national government being stronger than any other; or indeed one country having a bigger nuclear button than another – reference here to President Trump's nuclear button being bigger and in working order compared to that of Kim Jong Un of North Korea[23]. Armed conflicts between national governments must never take place again.

All nuclear weapons are to become the responsibility of the Earth Government and will be decommissioned as soon as practically possible.

And we must never allow children to be conscripted.

In terms of land mines - their production must be prohibited, stock piles destroyed together with the total destruction of all those already in use.

On the issue of terrorism and so called Islamic fundamentalism, I put it to every man, woman and child that the Qur'an states if your enemy inclines towards peace, incline also. The Christian Bible states "Blessed are the peacemakers".

An Earth Government would extend the hand of peace to all.

---

[23] https://twitter.com/realdonaldtrump/status/9483555557022420992?lang=en

CHAPTER 12 – EARTH RAPID REACTION AND EMERGENCY PLANNING

"Suffering anywhere concerns people everywhere". Kofi Annan

It is totally amazing how quickly humanity organizes rapid action strike forces in the pursuit of war, whether by a national government or through a coalition of countries, but so slow to deploy in the providing aid and assistance to people in need after a major disaster. We know full well that the first 12 to 24 hours in the immediate aftermath of any emergency are the most critical yet even in 2019, Hurricane Dorian which has brought devastation to the Bahamas has left 70,000 people[24] in need of urgent assistance. And yet it has taken days for even just a limited amount of relief to get through, not to mention the inability to provide any kind of temporary evacuation of survivors.

To resolve this issue and put right this injustice, an Earth Government would set up a Rapid Reaction and Emergency Planning Agency which will have the resources and money readily available when disaster strikes, instead of the current cap in hand situation, which has in the past had an over reliance upon aid agencies and donations. A Rapid Reaction and Emergency Planning Agency would be funded by using existing national Aid budgets and the use of current defence equipment and personnel. The Rapid Reaction and Emergency Planning Agency would provide that command and control function that is so often lacking, not only in a responsive way when disaster strikes but also pro-actively by putting plans into action to prevent and minimize the loss of life.

---

[24] https://www.theguardian.com/world/live/2019/sep/06/hurricane-dorian-latest-bahamas-carolinas-live-updates

I take great inspiration from the White Helmets who in Syria during its currently 8 year (as at 2019) conflict have provided, in the most dangerous circumstances, a truly remarkable service in search and rescue activities. The White Helmets, whilst ordinary men and women, who had very little resources, no or limited training were able to save thousands of lives during the horrendous Syrian conflict. I therefore propose we honour these individuals by naming the new Rapid Reaction and Emergency Planning Agency the White Helmets.

In its responsive form, this Rapid Reaction and Emergency Planning Agency will provide rapid reaction and deployment of technology and resources, including food, water, shelter, equipment, medical supplies and medical expertise in the form of doctors, medics and troops, during times of emergency to any country in need in any part of the world.

We must turn our current military strengths towards a direction of help rather than conflict. Therefore the strategy would to utilise around ten existing aircraft carriers plus additional support craft, and to recommission them for the deployment of aid and to equip them with fleets of rescue helicopters instead of fighter jets.

Moreover, in its pro-active form, it will prepare national countries for the effects of climate change. It would plan and forecast ahead where the greatest effects of our current climate catastrophe will hit the most. This Rapid Reaction and Emergency Planning Agency would see the amalgamation of all current aid agencies in order to utilise best practice and shared resources thus avoiding duplication.

As well as hurricane Dorian, this Rapid Reaction and Emergency Planning Agency clearly would have had a real and important impact for the USA during hurricane Katrina in 2005 where 1,836 people lost their lives[25]; the 2014 earthquake in China which incurred 617 causalities[26], the 2010 floods in Pakistan where it is reported that at least 2,000 people died[27], the several Ebola outbreaks across many African countries has killed thousands of people[28], and the fires across the World including Russia[29], Australia in the Black Saturday bushfires of 2009[30], and the Canadian wild fires in British Columbia in 2017[31].

[25] https://en.wikipedia.org/wiki/Hurricane_Katrina
[26] https://en.wikipedia.org/wiki/List_of_earthquakes_in_China
[27] https://en.wikipedia.org/wiki/List_of_floods_in_Pakistan
[28] https://www.cdc.gov/vhf/ebola/history/2014-2016-outbreak/index.html
[29] https://www.bbc.co.uk/news/world-europe-49182554
[30] https://www.historychannel.com.au/articles/the-worst-bushfires-in-australian-history/
[31] https://en.wikipedia.org/wiki/2017_British_Columbia_wildfires

CHAPTER 13 – EARTH COASTGUARD

"We do this job because every once in a while someone is out there without hope, desperately praying for their life, and we get to be the answer." Coast Guard (U.S.)

It often surprises me that considering 70% of planet earth is water and over 200 countries (circa 213 at last count) have a coastline, that we as a human race do not have a global and unified search and rescue coastguard already in place.

Clearly a quick check on the Internet will reveal that many countries do in fact have some form of a national coastguard tied to their national borders but provision is sporadic. Indeed, the US Coastguard as an example, whilst undertakes some splendid maritime life-saving work, is in reality more of a patrol organization under the Department of Homeland Security to prevent illegal immigration than it is with actually rescuing people in distress.

And as a side bar we need to view so called illegal immigration in a totally different light. Immigration today is caused by the 'push factors' that are driving people from their homeland. Let's be real here – no one really wants to leave to their country. But in our current global civilization we have created circumstances that are forcing people to move toin order to look for a better future. We need to even out the playing field so that people remain attracted to staying in their home country. This is not racist – this is ensuring our best resource (people) have the best opportunities to grow and develop in their country of birth.

An Earth Government would establish an Earth Coastguard which would be properly and centrally funded and fully resourced to save lives around the globe.

As well as being fully equipped with a new fleet of rescue boats it too in addition, and in a similar vein to the Rapid Reaction and Emergency Planning Agency, would have its own aircraft carriers, supporting vessels and fleet of helicopters, which would be strategically positioned around the planet and available and shared out to all countries dependent upon population size and specific requirements.

All new Earth Coastguard staff would be equipped with the latest technology and receive full and up to date training. A service truly fit for the 21st Century.

"Invention is the most important product of man's creative brain. The ultimate purpose is the complete mastery of mind over the material world, the harnessing of human nature to human needs." Nikola Tesla

It is absolutely obvious, as humanity marches towards becoming a space aged civilization, the necessity for us to have a global transport strategy. Our current transport infrastructure right across the globe is chaotic, fragmented, poorly resourced and is not in any real shape or form environmentally friendly. Humans, by their very nature, are social creatures and we need a new global transport system that enables not only local communities to be better connected but also a system that unites our countries like no other in our history.

A global Transport Strategy will provide a total commitment by the Earth Government in the production of new environmentally friendly cars, whether they be electric cars, hydrogen fuelled cars, or cars using ionic wind technology, with the eventual abolishment of petrol / diesel vehicles within the next 10 years.

Oil production will still be required for solar cell and plastic production. The price of oil needs to be fixed at around $100 per barrel so that oil producing countries are guaranteed a single fixed income over many years. However, oil will eventually be phased out and our economies will need time to make this fundamental shift from carbon intensive and carbon minimal.

In the short term while petrol/diesel cars are around an Earth Government will set a single pump price for petrol/diesel so that all consumers will pay the same whatever country they live in.

We need a new commitment to a fast, clean and efficient rail infrastructure within individual countries but also some kind of super-fast trans-continental travel. Recent research and development into Hyperloop technology[32] must be further explored and properly funded. Such technology offers humanity great possibilities in the transportation of people and goods at high speed but also reducing carbon dioxide and other harmful emissions.

---

[32] https://en.wikipedia.org/wiki/Hyperloop

"If you really believe that you're making a difference and that you can leave a legacy of better schools and jobs and safer streets, why would you not spend the money? The objective is to improve the schools, bring down crime, build affordable housing, [and] clean the streets."
Michael Bloomberg

An Earth Government will fund and manage a global House Building and Social Infrastructure Improvement Programme in partnership with and respecting the needs of local communities on a scale never witnessed before in every country.

It is, for example, an intolerable situation that over 1 billion people live in shanty towns around the world with children playing in sewerage. According to reliefweb.int around "70.8 million people live in refugee camps around the world and 37,000 people are forced to flee their homes every day due to conflict or persecution."[33] Enough is enough!

It will be a key aim of any future Earth Government to train and employ local people to build houses/refurbish existing houses, install proper sanitation, construct clean water pumps and maintain the new infrastructure in their local communities. An Earth Government will co-ordinate the excellent work already being undertaken by charities and Non Government Organizations (NGO's) to improve the lives of millions.

And there must be a new unified gold standard building regulation for all new buildings. I do not want a situation whereby through corruption

---

[33] https://reliefweb.int/report/world/world-refugee-day-2019

sub-standard or shoddy infrastructure is rapidly constructed that risks lives.

CHAPTER 16 – EARTH SPACE AGENCY

"Most certainly, some planets are not inhabited, but others are, and among these there must exist life under all conditions and phases of development." Nikola Tesla

It seems to me that nation states thrive when presented with a common goal or a concept to rally around. This was particularly true during World War two, where in fact both populations on either side of the axis or the allied forces, witnessed a strong sense of nationalistic belief in themselves and a steely determination to overcome.   I would like to propose that a new global strategic Earth Space Agency could re-create this same belief and determination but on a global scale, in which all of humanity could feel a sense of purpose in its mission to reach out into space and explore the stars.

Our current approach is dysfunctional and non-strategic, with significant sums of money being ploughed into cost centres which are being replicated by many countries. For example the US NASA and military space budget is around $48 billion, with Russia spending around $3 billion and China spending around $8.4 billion[34].   The European Space Agency budget for 2019 is just over $6 billion. Interestingly, the new National Space India Limited company is to have a budget of $1.45 billion[35]. The new Earth Space Agency would unify all existing national space organizations, including their people, resources, technology and funding and have a new central command with all countries represented with an equal voice.

---

[34] https://www.nextbigfuture.com/2019/07/chinas-space-budget-is-nearly-triple-russias-budget-but-far-less-than-usa.html
[35] https://economictimes.indiatimes.com/news/science/budget-2019-isro-open-for-business-new-commercial-arm-to-harness-economic-benefits-of-isro/articleshow/70085844.cms

The new global space agency will examine ways into developing futuristic technologies, including space gravity, zero carbon space travel, clearing space junk around our planet, the possibility of space agriculture, solar collectors, asteroid mining, and planetary defence from asteroids and the creation of an initial Martian space colony to begin the process of terra forming it. We also need to have bold ideas of building a super structure that would enable humanity to travel at speeds faster than light; although this may be some time away. This may be a rotating spherical object – rotating in order to create artificial gravity, or a more traditional linear forward moving vessel. Either would need to be large enough to carry thousands of people and stable to travel of significant fast speeds.

In terms of Mars, it is suggested that the costs of human travel and life support once there will be too high to make this feasible. I therefore propose humanity terraforms the planet first by introducing a vegetation and water in order to extend its current thin atmosphere. Such a development would not happen overnight this is clearly a 100 year plus project.

Moreover, we have to be very careful that we don't suddenly create a new form of human being. The gravity of Mars is 62% less than it is here on planet Earth. Anyone born on Mars will never be able to visit Earth as their skeleton would be crushed under the weight of our own gravity. Any new civilization on the red planet must accommodate and be supported by artificial gravity that matches Earth's.

It is clear the moon must be left alone from any kind of mining activity or for any other purpose for that matter. There are two main reasons for this. Firstly, its gravitational importance in controlling our tides and the internal navigation systems of many species is undeniable. The loss of the moon would have a seismic impact on humanity and across our global ecosystem. Secondly, if nation states or private companies are allowed to profit in any way from exploiting the moon's resources, no matter how valuable, it would inevitably lead to its eventual demise. In addition, any uncontrolled break-up of the lunar system could result in large bodies of rock descending to Earth causing an extinction level event similar to a meteor. The vastness of space means we don't need to destroy our own backyard just to further humanity. We need to be thinking much wider and utilizing the resources within the asteroid belt, on other planets and their moons by creating a new deep space mining operation that benefits all humanity and not destroy it.

Our planet cannot really support 7 billion people rising to 9 billion by the year 2100. Only a coherent space programme will alleviate such population pressures and at the same time assist with the survival of humankind.

Therefore, the long term goal of the Earth Space Agency will be the identification of an Earth 2 planet which can later be colonised. It may very well be necessary for us to establish a Space Fleet organization with its own Space Fleet academy. And whilst public investment will provide the main back bone of all exploration and security there must be private partnership in place in terms of ancillary support and the transportation of supplies. This is currently proving effective with Space X supplying the international space station, but the arrangement must never become a "them and us" scenario.

Whatever your thoughts are on this, it is very much evident that humanity's future belongs in space exploration light years away from our tiny planet Earth. Only an Earth Government can deliver this in a coherent way – uniting national governments and focusing on a global space programme and bringing prosperity, equality and opportunity to all.

"It's not how much we give but how much love we put into giving."
Mother Theresa.

I really applaud the excellent work carried out by all charitable organizations and in particular the large international global charities, the Non-Governmental Organizations (NGO's) and those working under the UN umbrella.

However, it seems to me that there is a lack of co-ordination, a lack of collaboration and no long term joined up strategy between them. An Earth Government would seek to provide an opportunity for all charities to link in to a new Strategic Forum where a longer term vision and a proper strategic plan can be devised to help sort out our planet's woes.

We should be thinking of combining resources where we can and using the skills in these organizations to the best of our abilities. Resources and funding should available that circumvents the need for emergency campaigns for donations. I'm not saying such donations are wrong – not at all, but when a disaster strikes the people affected need help straight away in a matter of hours not days or even weeks.

And in a sort of a perverse way, I would be delighted to put such organizations out of business for good. Wouldn't it be fantastic if we could work together and eliminate the need for such charities within the confines of a few decades.

"A society should be judged not by how it treats its outstanding citizens but by how it treats its criminals." Fyodor Dostoyevsky.

We need to re-think justice and law & order across our civilizations. The current arrangement in many countries is just not working. You've only got to look at how India has dealt with the violence against women in recent years.[36] And how protests have been handled by China in Hong Kong.[37]

An Earth Justice Agency will utilise the current infrastructure of the International Criminal Courts, but with far greater powers. It will provide a clear Earth Government Criminal Justice strategy which will once and for all establish Earth Law. Earth Law will replace current legislation of International law but with far greater authority. Earth Law would ensure that individuals are protected whilst living in a different country against alleged violations of local customs which the person may not have reasonably knew. It would ensure that those who commit crimes in a country will never escape prosecution by hiding in another.

An Earth Justice Agency will include the establishment of an Earth Police Force, which for the first time ever will witness a truly joined up law enforcement agency. Any future Earth Police Force must be truly representative of colour and gender and have its own code of conduct that eliminates or at least tries to eliminate as best it possible can any kind of corruption.

---

[36] https://www.theguardian.com/world/2019/aug/08/india-government-fails-to-act-on-violence-against-women-and-girls
[37] https://www.amnesty.org/en/latest/news/2019/09/hong-kong-protests-explained/

Our civilization requires a reasoned debate in relation to gun control. Events in the USA have demonstrated that much tougher regulations are needed in the purchasing and ownership of guns. Ideally, I would argue no civilian should have access to a weapon; however, I recognize the situation is not always as clear cut as that. What is for certain though is that the current situation cannot be maintained where so many innocent lives are lost on a daily basis. I would even go to the extent to say that I don't believe our Police forces should in the mainstream be armed. There is a place for specially trained armed units that must operate under a very strict code.

Recent events in some African countries and in India have witnessed the appalling rape of women and young girls, by individuals and by gangs. An Earth Government will stamp out this disgraceful crime by proposing total life sentences for offenders. And life would really mean for the rest of the perpetrators natural life.

A review must take place into the world's correctional / rehabilitative services and prison estate with the aim of finding a balance in our continued struggle between incarceration and community led rehabilitation.

CHAPTER 19 - IMPLEMENTATION

So how will all this be achieved? That is the six million dollar question isn't it. It can be achieved within just a few weeks, although the state of current world politics in this year of 2016 is not yet poised to make this leap. Based on where we are today, any future Earth Government could take 500 years to come into fruition. Ironically, it would probably take some kind of extra-terrestrial encounter, even an alien attack that would drive humanity close enough to establish an Earth Government, but by which time it would probably be too late. If this were ever going to be the case and we the foresight to see this as a possibility, then surely it would be in our best defensive interest to unite under one flag now sooner rather than later in order to prepare. Perhaps this should be our new political posture – prepare for the worst, and set humanity up ready for a planned attack – as the saying goes prepare in haste, repent at leisure.

Regardless though of how we think the implementation could happen, it could at this moment in time only be driven by the United Nations. Until that time comes we may well have to wait 500 years.

The emergence of an Earth Government will present itself as a fresh start for all humanity.

CHAPTER 20 - CONCLUSION

"Imagine all the people living life in peace. You may say I'm a dreamer, but I'm not the only one. I hope someday you'll join us, and the world will be as one." John Lennon

This paper represents a blueprint for the establishment of an Earth Government. Whilst it is recognized that this is no mean feat and will not happen overnight, it is proposed that it can be achieved within a relatively short period of time with the right political climate and will.

The question really is, as James Paul Warburg reported in 1950 - a point I alluded to right at the very beginning of this book, will this be a voluntary act or an enforced reality. Will humanity be motivated enough to create the green future we need or will the planet fight back and force our hand in the matter, as it were. The latter of course may not necessarily be peaceful either, with a certain prediction of conflict between nation states. It could even transpire that whilst the majority of countries subscribe to an Earth Government in an attempt to re-balance planet Earth, there may be those countries in the minority who do not – potentially a new 21st century cold war.

I would like to draw to a close with the statement that humanity has to unite as a species if we are to survive. We have to put our differences aside and accept our various cultures. An Earth Government must as a legal authority protect and preserve individual cultures, where, of course this does not harm living individuals or creatures. We have to do more to end racism, sexism, ageism or any other negative "ism" you can think of for that matter.

It seems strange that even now in the twenty first century no one or no country has suggested having a fifty year or even a hundred year strategy – a business plan if you like. An Earth Government would devise such a strategy for the planet with each country playing its part to deliver this. It is clear that humanity and our planet, because of human activity, faces many challenges. Our priorities must focus on reducing as fast and as practicably possible the amount we pollute. We must strive for clean air, clean water (that is a clean hydrological system including oceans, seas, estuaries and rivers), clean soil and an investment in to re-stocking our biological and species diversity. We have to reduce and clear our plastic pollution and embark on this as if we are on a wartime footing. We are only custodians on this planet – that means having a level of responsibility to protect and preserve species diversity for future generations to enjoy and benefit.

I know this is not going to be easy and this will represent some hard reading for many people, especially those of us and I include myself in this bracket, who currently live quite comfortable lives in our western democracies. What we have to remember is that extremes of anything are bad – so in politics, for example, extremes on the left or the right are dangerous societal movements. In the same way extreme levels of greenhouse gases in our atmosphere will cause extremes and volatility in our planetary weather systems. We've seen so many of these over recent years and yes these will become the normal in the future. In the same vein if we have too little greenhouse gases in our atmosphere our climatic patterns will become much colder – and we've seen this in the past as ice ages. What we have to strive for is a balance – to restore the planet's own natural equilibrium.

www.ingramcontent.com/pod-product-compliance
Lightning Source LLC
Chambersburg PA
CBHW060222290526
45789CB00003B/1368